Contents

INTRODUCTION

A short guide to the highlights of Scotland's North Coast 500 route – driving Anticlockwise (from East to West)

When we decided to drive the North Coast 500 route, we spent hours on the internet reading people's blogs and using Google to search for the recommended trip highlights. We wanted to find out the best places to see en-route and activities that interested us such as hiking and good places to canoe. We wanted to make sure we allowed enough time, and carefully selected our overnight stops to ensure we didn't feel rushed or come home feeling we had missed anything.

This short guide aims to put into one place all the information we spent hours searching for on the internet, covering the highlights of the route, with suggestions and recommendations for short walks, hikes and canoe trips.

What this guide *doesn't* include is accommodation listings – existing places close and new places open up all the time. We have, however, listed some of the camping and campervan sites in key locations along the route. It is worth bearing in mind that many of the campsites close for the autumn & winter, however, we have indicated the ones that are open year-round.

Before you go – planning hints and tips

- To give you an idea of what to expect, you can watch our video on YouTube by by typing in this URL: https://www.youtube.com/watch?v=OR7E8-yJEl8&feature=youtu.be

- The route is 500 miles long, and although some people have done it in 4 or 5 days, we recommend allowing yourself at least 7 – 10 days to allow yourself time to enjoy some activities such as hiking

- A useful map can be picked up at the Tourist Information Centres, or it can be downloaded and printed from the NC500 website using this URL: https://www.northcoast500.com/wp-content/uploads/2018/07/NC500-Official-Map.pdf

- Pre-book your accommodation or campsites if possible, but particularly from Easter until around mid-end September (This is not as important from around October to March, however, be aware that many of the campsites and accommodations may be closed for the season)

- In our opinion there is no good or bad time to go – the weather in Scotland is fairly unpredictable year-round, however, we enjoyed the very quiet "off" season (end October into mid-November) and we were blessed with fine weather for most of our trip

- This guide was written to advise you of the route's highlights, however, we recommend that you spend a bit of time thinking about what else you would like to do (e.g. hiking, golfing, canoeing, etc.) and based on that, where would be most suitable for your overnight stays

- Consider spending more than one night in some places. Within this guide are some suggestions. For example, there are some great walks around Assynt and Torridon, however, if you are a golfer you may want some extra time on the East Coast to experience some of the famous Scottish golf courses

- If you choose to make a side trip to any of the islands, allow some "contingency" time for weather-related ferry cancellations or disruptions (our return Pentland ferry from Orkney was cancelled, however, we were fortunate to get a place on the Northlink one, which sails a different route, otherwise we would have lost a day on the NC500)

- Decide whether you prefer to travel anticlockwise (East to West, as we did) or clockwise (West to East) – for us, the anticlockwise direction was great as we finished the trip with the most stunning scenery (saved the best for last!)

- If you are driving up to Inverness, think about where might make a nice stop (or stops) en-route – we travelled from Glasgow and stopped overnight in Killin on the way so that we could enjoy and photograph the beautiful Perthshire autumn foliage

- Check websites such as 5pm.co.uk, Groupon and Itison for hotel deals along the route, especially in the off-season there are often quite a few deals to be had

- Pack for all seasons, even in summer, and particularly if you plan any hill walks, make sure you have plenty of warm and waterproof clothing and good footwear (*Tip*: in Scotland, we never travel without our wellies – for non-Scots, that's rubber boots!)

- Unless you are travelling out of season, bring plenty of midge (insect) repellent.

- There are some awesome beaches and bays along the West coast that are great for canoeing in calm weather – we bought an Intex inflatable double canoe from Amazon and had great fun paddling about in it!

- For hotels, bed & breakfast and self-catering we recommend using Airbnb and Booking.com

THE EAST COAST - Inverness to John O'Groats: 120 miles and approximately 2 hours 45 minutes driving time

INVERNESS (IN & AROUND)

We would recommend visiting the Tourist Information Centre on the pedestrianised High Street. There you can find out what's on, book (for example) a cruise on Loch Ness, pick up maps, etc.

In the city itself, you may also consider a visit to Inverness Castle which overlooks the River Ness and currently houses the Sheriff Court. Note that at present only the north tower is accessible (as a viewpoint), though this may change in the future as the court is due to move to another location.
Then take a stroll along the river to the Ness Islands, which are about 20 minutes walk south of the castle. The islands are linked to each other and the riverbank by Victorian footbridges.

About 6 miles outside of the city, you can head to Culloden Battlefield, the site of the final battle of the Jacobite rebellion. From there, follow the signs for the Clava Cairns, prehistoric burial cairns dating back about 4,000 years. They are a couple of miles from Culloden battlefield.

Urquhart Castle, on the banks of Loch Ness, is about a half-hour away, heading south on the A82.

THE BLACK ISLE (A SHORT SIDE TRIP)

There are quite a few attractions worth considering on the Black Isle, a short diversion off the main NC500 route. Despite its name, the Black Isle isn't an island at all, but a peninsula which is surrounded by water on three sides – the Cromarty Firth, the Beauly Firth and the Moray Firth.

Head out to Chanonry Point (about 15 miles from Inverness) to try your luck at spotting the bottlenose dolphins. This is considered one of the best places in the country to view them, often close to the shore. But bear in mind that the best time to view them is as the tide is coming in, about an hour after low tide. The dolphins are there throughout the year but are more often sighted in the summer months hunting for salmon. The harbour porpoises are also present year-round, and minke whales can sometimes be seen from around March to October.

A couple of miles from Chanonry Point, just outside the village of Rosemarkie, you will find the Fairy Glen RSPB Reserve. There is a car park on the right as the road leaves the village in the direction of Cromarty (currently free, but donations gratefully accepted). There is an easy walk up a wooded glen, with two pretty waterfalls at the end of the path. The distance is around 3 kilometres for the round trip, you should allow around one hour.

Heading back to the A9 to rejoin the NC500 route, a few miles before the A9, near the village of Munlochy there are a couple of other attractions you may like to visit. A couple of miles through the village is the Black Isle Brewing Company, who do tours and tastings of their organic, home-grown beer. On the main A832, there is the somewhat bizarre Clootie Well. As you approach or drive by, you will see bits of cloth and clothing hanging from the trees. It all dates back to an ancient tradition, where pilgrims would come to make offerings, usually in the hope of having an illness cured. Today the tradition continues, however, as it has now got quite out of hand, there was a "clean up" in progress while we were visiting.

TAIN (35 miles and approximately 50 minutes driving time from Inverness)

Features both a golf course and the Glenmorangie whisky distillery (tours and tastings available), so you are spoilt for choice if either or both of these things interest you! There are several more golf courses and a few distilleries as you travel along the East coast.

Tip: For the whisky lovers, distilleries such as Dalmore (located in Alness, about 20 miles north of Inverness) and Old Pulteney (in Wick, about 16 miles south of John O'Groats) offer tours and tastings.

For golfers, to mention only a few of the east coast courses, you have the famous Royal Dornoch championship course in Dornoch, the Golspie golf course near Dunrobin Castle with its mix of links, heath and parkland and the links course in Brora. All the aforementioned courses lie along a 17 mile stretch of the NC500.

DUNROBIN CASTLE, GOLSPIE (approximately 19 miles and 30 minutes driving time from Tain)

The stunning Dunrobin Castle, which overlooks the Moray Firth, has been home to the Dukes and Earls of Sutherland since the 13th century. The castle and gardens are open from 1st April to 31st October. A visit to the castle includes a falconry display from April to September, check the website for up to date details (dunrobincastle.co.uk).

You can walk to the beach for an excellent view of the castle without having to pay to go in, so unless you want a look inside the castle or gardens, this is your best option. Use the free car park and take the path down past the castle grounds to the beach.

DUNROBIN CASTLE

BRORA BEACH (approximately 5 miles and 10 minutes driving time north of Dunrobin Castle)

At Brora there lies a long stretch of sandy beach bordering on the golf course, so it's a great place to make a short stop to stretch your legs. It also makes for nice photo opportunities. When we were there, we were lucky enough to catch this full rainbow.

RAINBOW OVER BRORA GOLF COURSE

WHALIGOE STEPS (approximately 39 miles and 60 minutes driving time from Brora)

The Whaligoe Steps are a little hard to find as they are currently not signposted, but it is worth the effort. The road to them is exactly opposite the sign for the Cairn of Get, so watch out for that. There is parking available, but spaces are very limited.

There are over 300 steps which take you down from the clifftop to a naturally formed harbour with a rocky beach, that sits in between two sea cliffs. This was once a landing place for fishing boats and the steps were then used by fisherwomen to haul up the creels of herring. The scenery as you walk down, and even more so once you reach the bottom, is quite dramatic. You may have read or heard that you have to be very careful to use the steps, but they are currently under repair and we felt perfectly safe. A bonus when we visited, was the mother seal and pup that were there, the mother bobbing about in the sea keeping watch on her pup, and the pup lying on the rocks on the beach. We visited at the end of October, which is a good time of year for seeing seal pups, not only at Whaligoe but at many locations along the NC500.

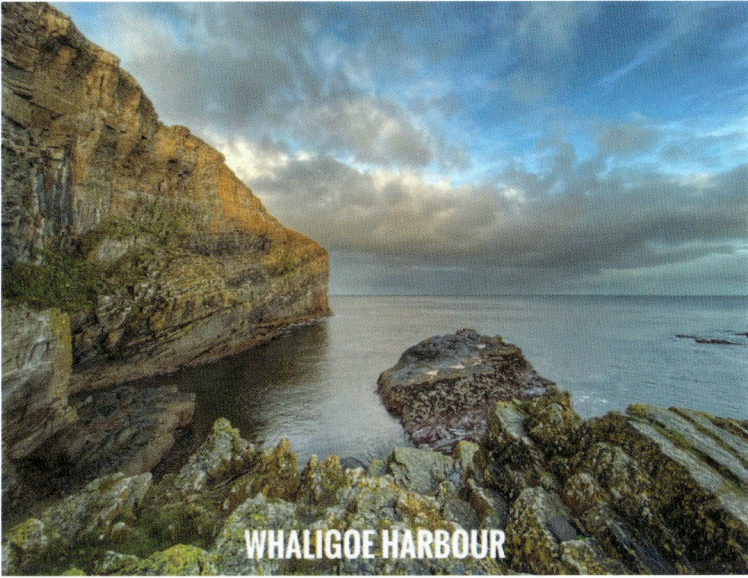
WHALIGOE HARBOUR

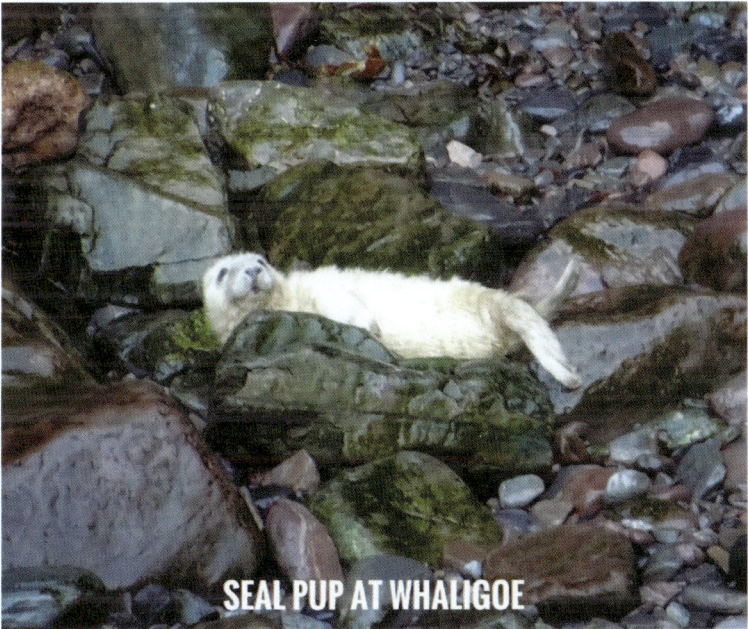
SEAL PUP AT WHALIGOE

JOHN O'GROATS - DUNCANSBY HEAD & THE SEA
STACKS (approximately 25 miles and 40 minutes
driving time north of the Waligoe Steps)

Just outside of JohnO'Groats, take the single track road to
Duncansby Head, park in the car park (free at the time of
writing) and follow the path for around 20 minutes or so
to view the dramatic Duncansby Sea Stacks. Another great
photo spot and a good opportunity for a short stroll to
stretch your legs.

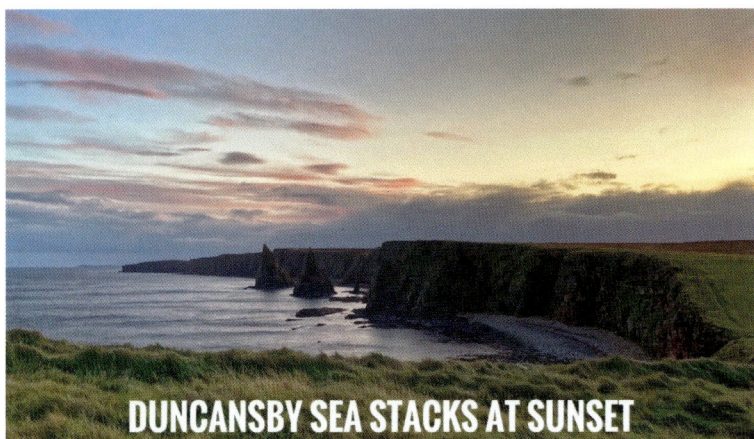
DUNCANSBY SEA STACKS AT SUNSET

THE NORTH COAST - John O'Groats to Durness: 90 miles and approximately 2 hours 30 minutes driving time

GILLS BAY PORT (approximately 4 miles and 10 minutes driving time from John O'Groats)

Gills Bay is mainly of interest if you are making a side trip to Orkney. The route is run by Pentland Ferries, sails to St Margarets Hope and takes approximately one hour.

DUNNET HEAD & DUNNET BAY (approximately 12 miles and 20 minutes driving time from John O'Groats to Dunnet Bay and approximately a further 5 miles and 15 minutes drive out to Dunnet Head one-way)

Dunnet Bay consists of almost 2 miles of sandy beach backed by dunes.
There is a 10.5-mile coastal walk from Dwarwick Pier at Dunnet Bay, which takes you along the cliffs to Dunnet Head. Take care when walking along the unprotected cliff edges. Parking is available at the start of the walk. If you are interested in reading more about this walk you can find a detailed walk description on the Walk Highlands

website.

In good weather, Dunnet Bay is quite sheltered and can be a good spot for a swim or canoe paddle. It is also popular with surfers when the winds are high, so please check the local weather forecast.

Dunnet Head is the most northerly point on the British mainland. On a clear day you can see over to the Orkney Islands, and along the north shore to Duncansby Head to the east and Cape Wrath to the west.

There is a lighthouse and an RSPB nature reserve at Dunnet Head. You can view many species of seabirds, including puffins (in spring and early summer) from the viewpoints on the cliffs.

For gin lovers, there is a distillery at Dunnet Bay (Dunnet Bay Distillers) famous for their "Rock Rose Gin". Tours and tastings are available.

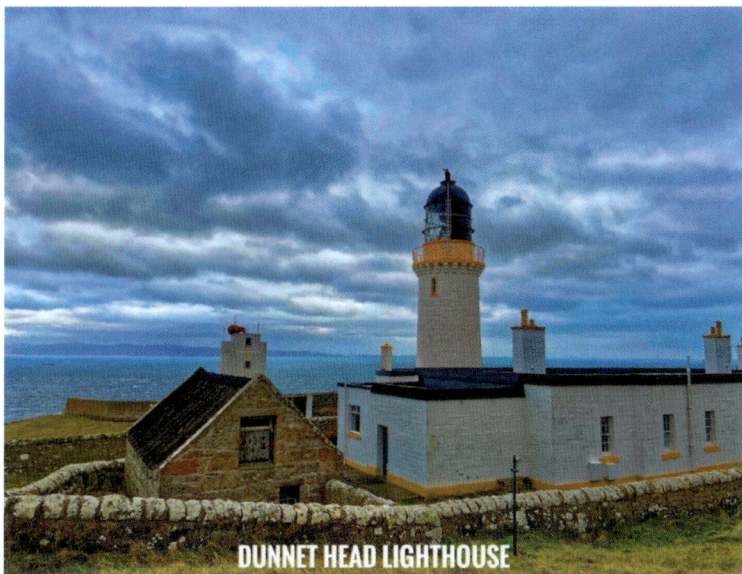
DUNNET HEAD LIGHTHOUSE

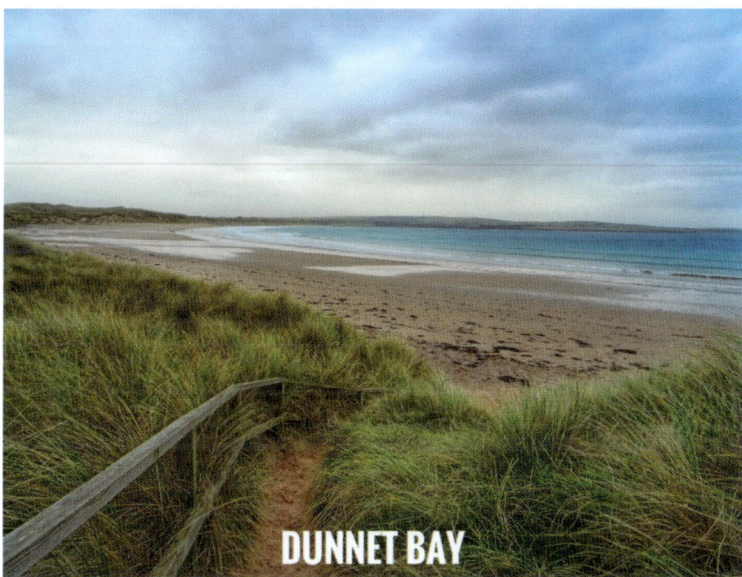
DUNNET BAY

THURSO (approximately 8 miles and 15 minutes driving time from Dunnet Bay)

Thurso is the most northerly town in mainland Scotland and is the best place to stock up on groceries if you are self-catering. There is a Tesco, Lidl and a Co-op. There is also a selection of local shops, cafes, bars and restaurants.

SCRABSTER (approximately 2 miles and 5 minutes driving time from Thurso)

From Scrabster, you can get a Northlink ferry to Orkney, the route sails to Stromness on Mainland Orkney and takes around 1 hour and 30 minutes.

KYLE OF TONGUE (approximately 42 miles and 1 hour 10 minutes driving time from Thurso)

The whole north coast route is very scenic, with mountains and beautiful beaches. The Kyle of Tongue is a shallow sea loch, crossed by a causeway and bridge. The loch and its surrounding countryside have been classed as a National Scenic Area.

A popular hill walk and the most northerly Munro, Ben Hope, is not far from here. To get to the start of this walk you need to continue on the NC500 for around 7 miles after crossing the causeway, then take a short diversion left along the length of Loch Hope and continue to the car park in Strathmore. Further details on the walk can be found on the Walk Highlands website.

If you are looking for a short walk, you can head into Tongue village, and walk up to the ruined Castle Varrich, which you will see as you drive towards the Kyle of Tongue. This short walk takes around one hour.

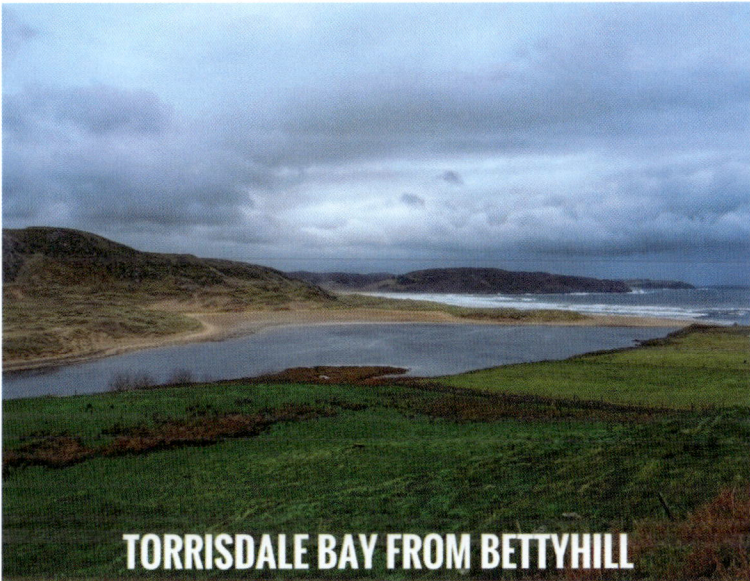

TORRISDALE BAY FROM BETTYHILL

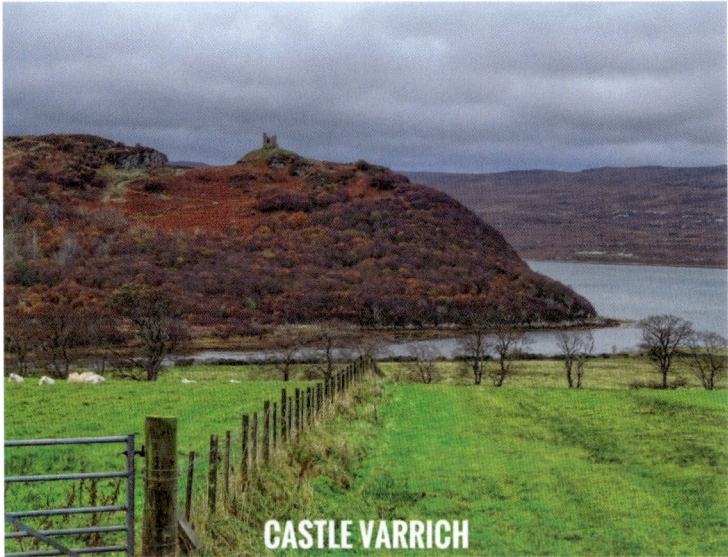

CASTLE VARRICH

LOCH ERIBOLL (approximately 11 miles and 20 minutes driving time from Kyle of Tongue)

Loch Eriboll is another lovely sea loch. In the loch, the much-photographed Ard Neackie is linked to the east shore by a thin strip of beach. Driving around the loch is delightful.

RISPOND BAY & CAENNABIENNE BEACH (en-route to Durness from Loch Eriboll)

Once you have gone around Loch Eriboll, and before you reach Durness, you may wish to make a stop at the photogenic Rispond Bay and Ceannabeinne Beach.

DURNESS (approximately 18 miles and 40 minutes driving time from the eastern shore of Loch Eriboll)

As you approach Durness, the first major attraction you will pass is Smoo Cave. There is a car park and a relatively steep walk down (via steps) to the cave entrance. The cave is floodlit inside and has wooden walkways over the water. Inside the cave is a 20-metre high waterfall with a viewing platform.

Stunning beaches in and near Durness include Sango Sands (which also has a year-round campsite, though not all facilities are open during the off-season) and Balnakeil Bay, 5 minutes out of the village. Our personal favourite is Balnakeil, with huge sandy beaches backed by massive dunes. Next to the main beach is a nine-hole golf course and a ruined church.

For chocolate lovers, Cocoa Mountain at Balnakeil comes highly recommended and many people rave about their hot chocolate.

Durness is a place where we would recommend spending a couple of nights, particularly in good weather, to enjoy the beaches or a round of golf.

BALNAKEIL BAY

THE WEST COAST & BACK TO INVERNESS –

Durness to Inverness: Approximately 280 miles and approximately 8 hours driving time

OLDSHOREMORE BEACH & SANDWOOD BAY (both reached by coming off the NC500 at Rhiconich, which is approximately 14 miles and 25 minutes driving time from Durness)

A very worthwhile detour off the NC500 is Oldshoremore Beach, which is approximately 6.5 miles and 15 minutes driving time from Rhiconich, heading towards (and beyond) Kinlochbervie.

This stunning beach is easily accessible, you can park next to it and just walk a short distance over the dunes to reach the beach. We thought this beach was amazing, and it's a great option if you don't have time to walk to Sandwood Bay, which is said to be one of the most beautiful (and remote) beaches on the Scottish mainland.

If time allows for a hike of around 8 miles / 4 hours (return), then continue to drive to the car park at Blairmore, another couple of miles on, and from there you can start the hike to the remote and beautiful Sandwood Bay.

OLDSHOREMORE BEACH

KYLESKU BRIDGE (approximately 20.5 miles and 30 minutes driving time from Rhiconich)

Passing the pretty village of Scourie along the way, you will shortly reach the impressive Kylesku Bridge, which crosses Loch a' Chairn Bhain. It is definitely worth stopping to get out of your car before and/or after the bridge to stretch your legs and take some photographs.

There is also a hotel in the village, situated on the banks of Loch Glendhu, should you wish to stop for lunch or overnight. Just look for the sign for the Kylesku Hotel.

KYLESKU BRIDGE

DRUMBEG LOOP (A worthwhile scenic detour taken by turning right – if travelling anticlockwise - off the NC500 and onto the B869)

This loop is around 30 miles long assuming you rejoin the NC500 again near Ardvreck Castle. The B869 stretch (about 20 miles) is a single track road with passing places. Please note that it is not considered suitable for motorhomes or towed caravans, though small campervans should be ok.

Make sure you stop at the Drumbeg Viewpoint to admire and photograph the view!

After the Drumbeg viewpoint, there are some beautiful beaches to visit.

ASSYNT MOUNTAINS FROM THE DRUMBEG LOOP

ACHMELVICH, CLACHTOLL & CLASHNESSIE BEACHES (all on the Drumbeg Loop)

You will pass by Clashnessie and Clachtoll beaches, with Achmelvich being a mile or so off the Loop road. Please don't miss it, it is worth the extra couple of miles drive!

These beaches are beautiful with white sand and turquoise sea. Our personal favourites are Clachtoll, which can be good for sunsets, and Achmelvich which is great for a wee canoe paddle.

While you are at Achmelvich beach you can go hunting for the tiny "Hermit's Castle", there is no track to it, so it can be a little tricky to find - just head out over the higher ground from the left-hand side of the beach.

ACHMELVICH BEACH

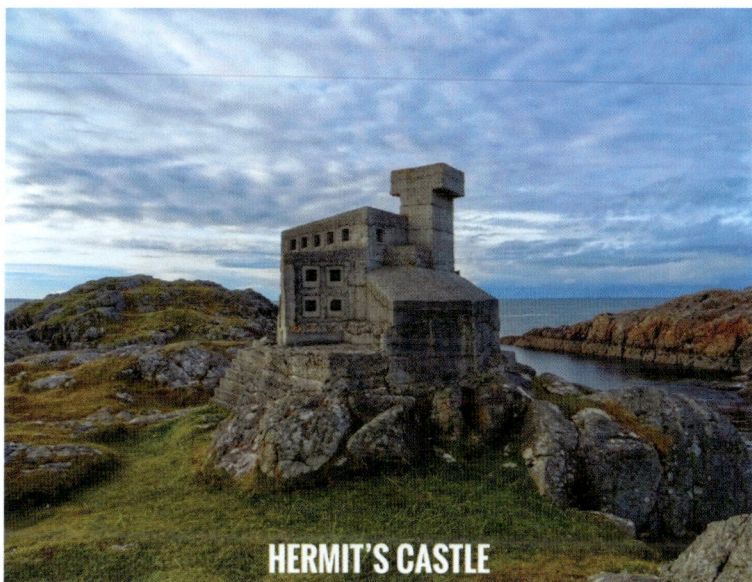

HERMIT'S CASTLE

CLACHTOLL BEACH

LOCHINVER (approximately 25 miles and 1 hour 10 minutes driving time from the Kylesku Bridge via the Drumbeg Loop, OR 18 miles and 30 minutes driving time via the NC500 and the A837)

There is so much to see and do around Lochinver that we would recommend spending at least a couple of nights. The views from Lochinver and Baddidarroch (just over the water) are spectacular. We saw some stunning sunrises from our accommodation in Baddidaroch.

If you enjoy canoeing or kayaking there are the bays mentioned above at Achmelvich, Clachtoll and Clashnessie. We also took our canoe out from the marina in Lochinver on a calm day. We asked the harbour staff if we could launch from the pontoon and it was no problem.

Ardvreck Castle and the walks mentioned below are also within easy reach of Lochinver, as is the long and popular hike up Sulvien.

Finally, the "pie shop" (Lochinver Larder) has to be given a mention, as their pies have become quite famous, justifiably so. It is now much more than just a pie shop, it operates a licensed restaurant too, so you can sit in or take out. They make both savoury and sweet pies.

LOCHINVER

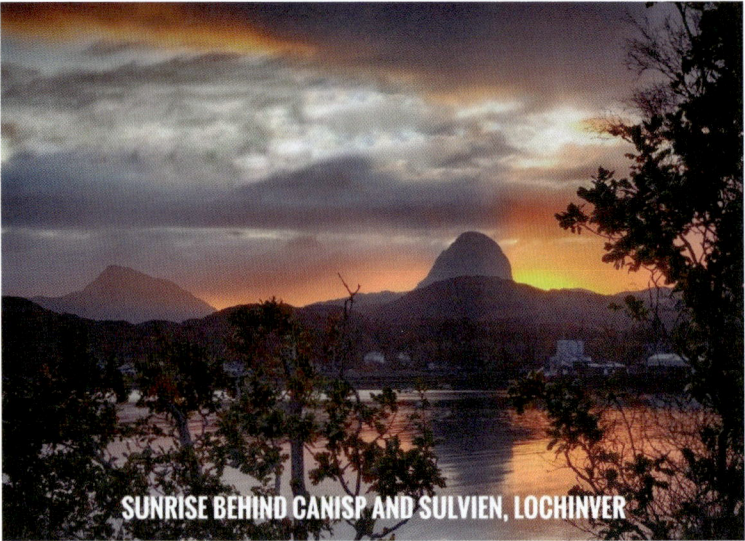
SUNRISE BEHIND CANISP AND SULVIEN, LOCHINVER

ARDVRECK CASTLE (approximately 11 miles and 15 minutes driving time from Lochinver)

This ruined castle sits on a promontory on the shores of Loch Assynt. Access is easy via a very short walk from the parking area, which also has interesting information boards detailing its history. The ruined mansion Calda House is also a short walk along the road from the parking area.

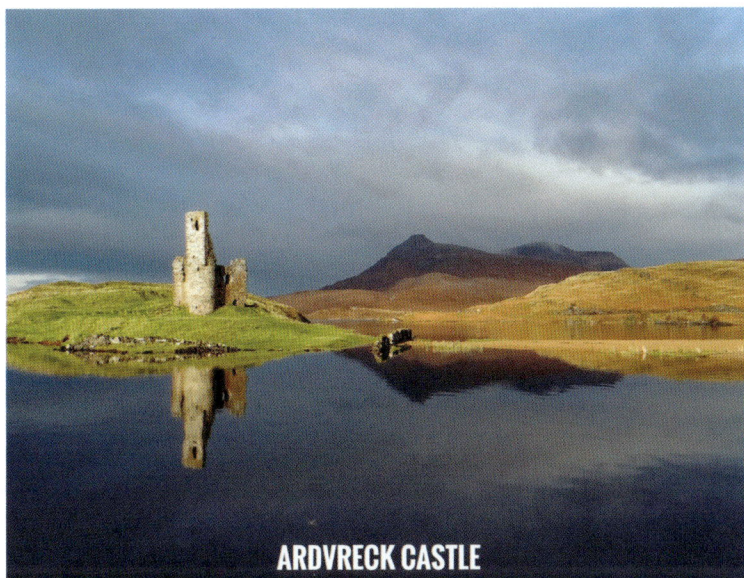
ARDVRECK CASTLE

THE BONE CAVES HIKE (approximately 4 miles and 5 minutes driving time from Ardvreck castle)

Look for the Allt nan Uamh car park a few miles past Inchnadamph.

This short and relatively easy walk of just under 3 miles can be done partially as a circuit. It took us around 2 hours at a leisurely pace, with photo stops and time exploring the caves.

It is not a difficult walk, but there is a steep section leading to and from the caves, so just take a little extra care there. Bones of wild animals such as lynx, reindeer, brown bear and even polar bear were found within in the four caves.

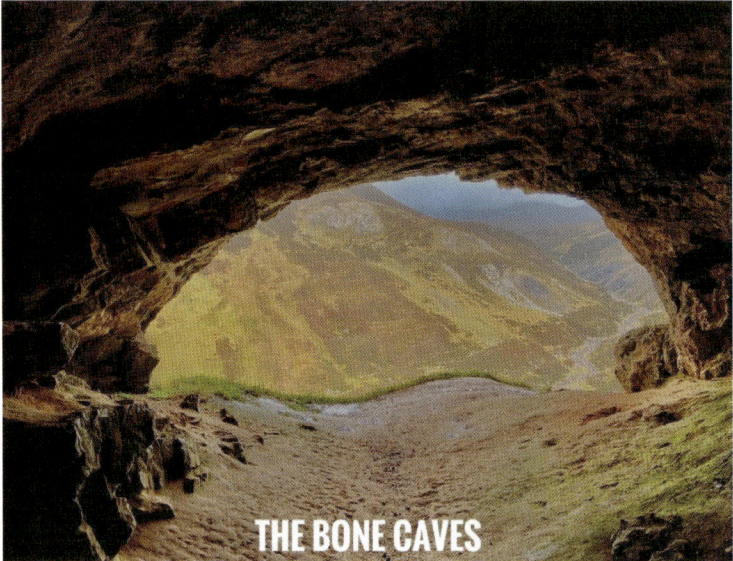
THE BONE CAVES

STAC POLLAIDH HIKE (approximately 16.5 miles and 30 minutes driving time from the Bone Caves car park)

This is a stunning and relatively short hike, with 360-degree views that may well be impossible to beat! If you were to do only one hike on your NC500 trip, we would recommend this one (weather permitting).

Tip: If you were staying in Lochinver and have already visited Advreck Castle and the Bone Caves, you have the option instead of reaching Stac Pollaidh by taking the unnamed single track road from Lochinver out towards (and beyond) Strathan and Inverkirkaig. This scenic route will take you approximately 15 miles and 45 minutes of driving time.

The hike took us a little less than 3 hours at a leisurely pace, with plenty of photo stops. It is not a difficult hike, but there are some steep sections. You can either make a circuit or come back the same way.

Should you wish to climb to the summit please make sure you read the information on the Walk Highlands website, as a high degree of scrambling ability is required. We hiked only to the saddle, as we were not experienced or comfortable enough to do any scrambling, especially with the gusts of wind that were blowing across the top!

CUL MOR AND CUL BEAG FROM STAC POLLAIDH HIKE

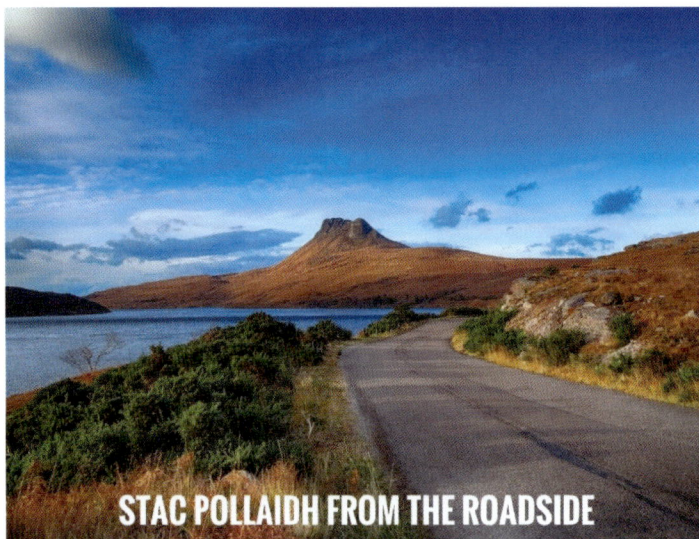
STAC POLLAIDH FROM THE ROADSIDE

ULLAPOOL (approximately 15 miles and 30 minutes driving time from the Stac Pollaidh car park OR 21 miles and 30 minutes driving time from the Bone Caves car park)

Ullapool is a small, pretty fishing town that sits on the shores of Loch Broom. It is also a jumping-off point for getting to the Outer Hebrides. The ferry goes over to Stornaway on the stunning Isles of Lewis and Harris (separate names but one landmass), a side trip very worth considering if you have the time.
Like Lochinver, there is plenty to see and do if you were to base yourself here for a couple of nights or more.

There are plenty of accommodation options, shops, bars

and restaurants. Just some of the activities available are boat trips, golf and kayaking.

In town, there is a petrol station to fuel up and a Tesco supermarket where you can stock up on provisions.

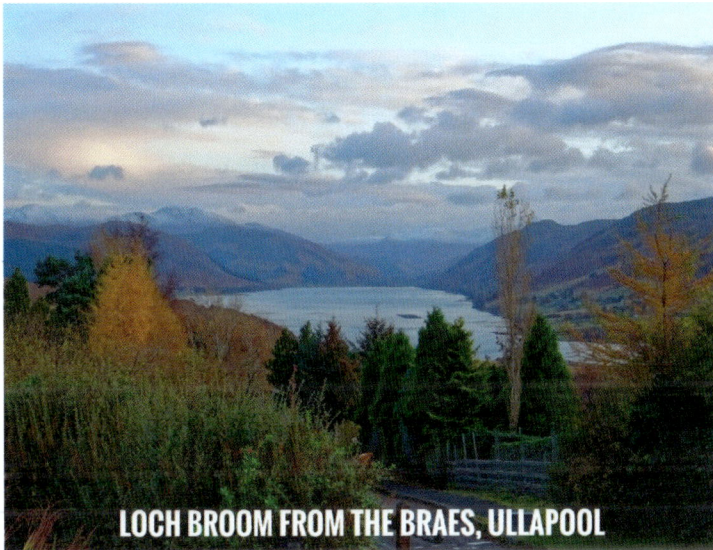

LOCH BROOM FROM THE BRAES, ULLAPOOL

CORRIESHALLOCH GORGE / FALLS OF MEASACH (approximately 12 miles and 20 minutes driving time from Ullapool)

Looked after by the National Trust, there is car parking available at this nature reserve. The river Droma flows through the gorge which is about a mile long and 60 metres deep. You can walk over the suspension bridge to look at the rushing river and 45-metre falls. There are short woodland trails, one with a view looking over to Loch Broom in the distance.

Allow yourself around 30 minutes to enjoy this nature reserve.

WEST COAST BEACHES – GRUINARD BAY / MELLON UDRIGLE / AULTBEA / POOLEWE / GAIRLOCH (approximately 44 miles and 1 hour 5 minutes driving time from Corrieshalloch to Gairloch)

The beaches along this section of the west coast all make for popular stops, even if just to get out the car to take photographs or have a walk on the beach. In the right conditions, it would be worth considering one or more of them for a canoe paddle.

There are a few campsites along this section, as well as hotels and B&B's etc. It is a popular area for an overnight stop.

GAIRLOCH BEACHES

TORRIDON (approximately 30 miles and 50 minutes driving time from Gairloch)

The NC500 turns inland after Gairloch and takes you along most of the length of Loch Maree, before turning back out towards the coast at Upper Loch Torridon.

We had hoped to get our canoe out at Loch Maree, but it was too windy, however, if you enjoy canoeing or kayaking, then in good conditions it would be worth considering.

This part of the drive is through remote and spectacular countryside, with views of the Torridon mountains at every turn.

For hill walkers, you may wish to allow time to climb one of these spectacular mountains. Popular walks include the Bienn Eighe Mountain Trail for a shorter (approximately 4 mile) walk or the Bienn Eighe Western Summits for a longer traverse (approximately 11 miles). We also met some people who raved about the walk up Bienn Damh (approximately 7.5 miles). There are lots of possibilities and the best idea is to have a look on the Walk Highlands website:
https://www.walkhighlands.co.uk/torridon/torridon.shtml

BEINN EIGHE, TORRIDON

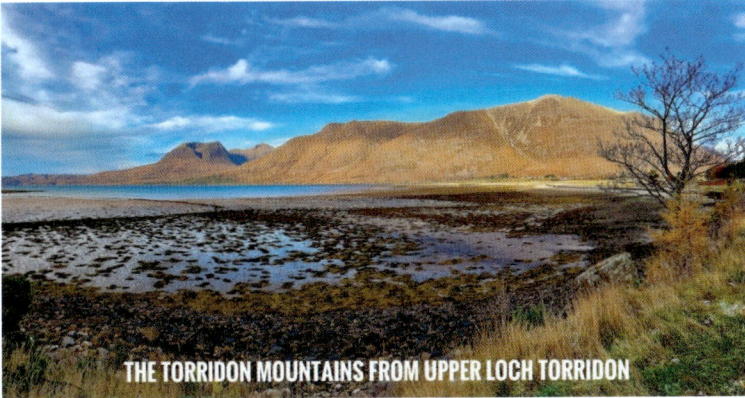
THE TORRIDON MOUNTAINS FROM UPPER LOCH TORRIDON

SHEILDAIG (approximately 7.5 miles and 15 minutes driving time from Torridon)

A beautiful little fishing village on the banks of Loch Sheildaig, especially picturesque when viewed across the loch from the Applecross Peninsula. The village has a shop and a hotel, plus a cafe should you just wish to stop in this lovely place for a cup of coffee.

APPLECROSS VILLAGE VIA THE APPLECROSS PENINSULA (approximately 25 miles and 1 hour driving time from Sheildaig)

A beautiful drive, with some great photo opportunities along the way!
One of the classic photo stops is the red-roofed white cottage at Inverbain, looking over Loch Sheildaig.

If you like smoked fish or smoked cheese, make sure to stop at the Applecross Smokehouse, just before Kenmore.

Continuing on you will pass plenty of other nice photo stops, including the view from Kalnakill looking out towards the Isle of Skye and the Cuillin mountain range. Along this stretch you may also have a forced photo stop, should the highland cattle decide to block the road!

About 4 miles before you get to Applecross, be sure to stop at Sands beach, a lovely beach backed by high dunes, again looking over to the Isle of Skye. You will often see the youngsters "surfing" down the dunes!

Applecross village is tiny, but it is another place that we would recommend to stop for a couple of nights, as there is plenty to explore around the area, such as a walk to Ard Ban and Coral beaches near Culduie (Ard Ban beach has great views over to the Isle of Skye and the Cuillin mountain range).

The village has a pub, the Applecross Inn, which also serves great food. The closest shop is about 2 miles south of the village.

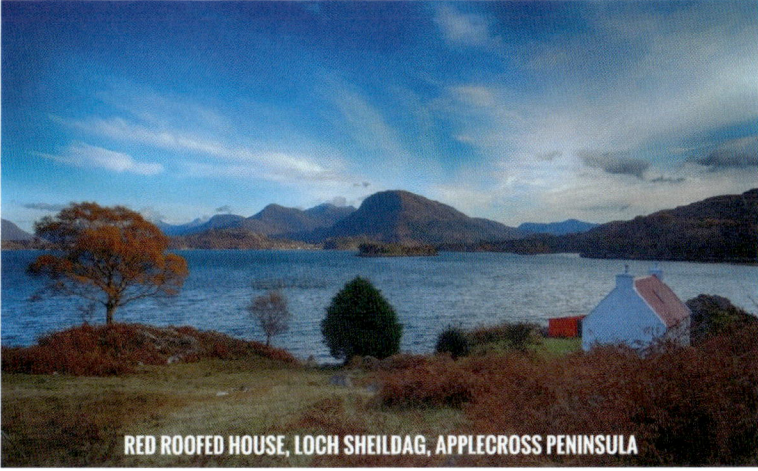

RED ROOFED HOUSE, LOCH SHEILDAG, APPLECROSS PENINSULA

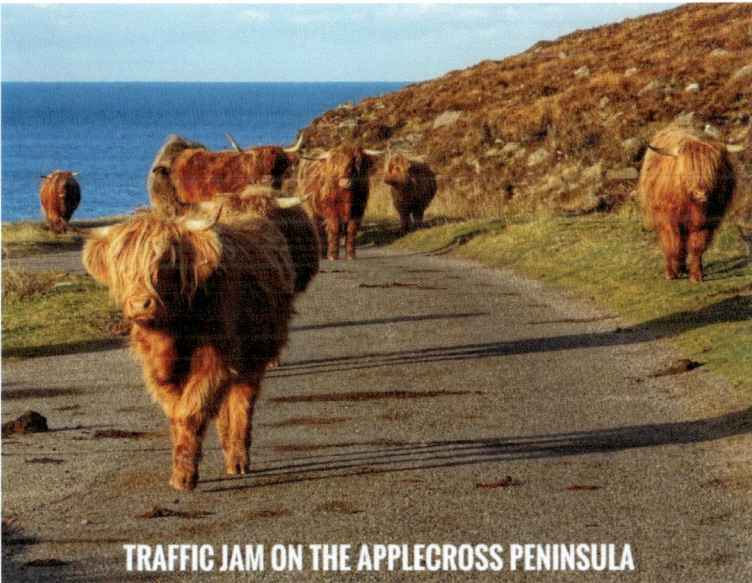

TRAFFIC JAM ON THE APPLECROSS PENINSULA

STAG AT APPLECROSS BAY

BEALACH NA BA "PASS OF THE CATTLE"
(approximately 11 miles and 35 minutes driving
time to cross the Bealach Na Ba from Applecross
to Tornapress)

One of the most dramatic roads in the country, rising to
around 2,000 feet above sea level with tremendous views
over to the Isle of Skye from the summit, this single track
road full of hairpin bends, is one of the highlights of the
NC500. Please note that this road is often closed in winter
conditions, and even in good conditions, it is not suitable
for large motorhomes or caravans.

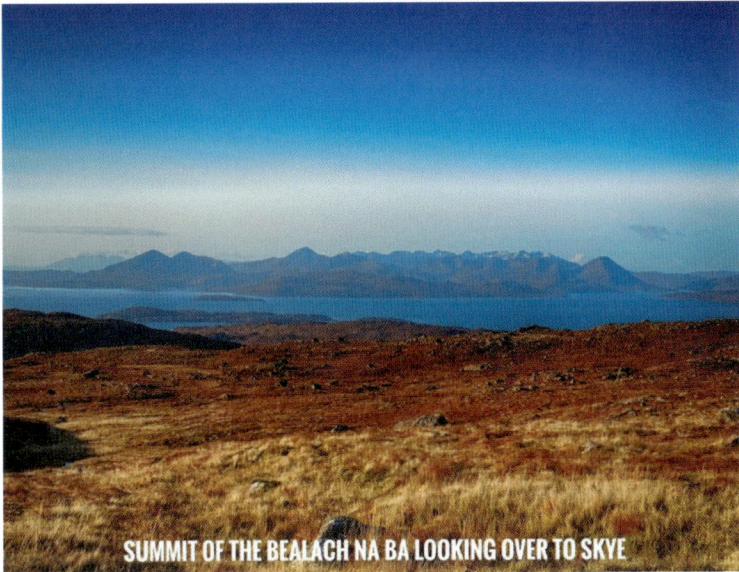
SUMMIT OF THE BEALACH NA BA LOOKING OVER TO SKYE

ROGIE FALLS (approximately 48 miles and 1 hour 5 minutes driving time from Tornapress, after crossing the Bealach Na Ba)

A picturesque place to stop and stretch your legs on the last leg of the NC500 as you back to Inverness. There are a couple of forest walks, both take in the viewpoint and suspension bridge overlooking the falls. During August and September, there is a good chance of seeing the salmon leaping upstream.

Allow 30 to 60 minutes to visit. It is a short walk on the Salmon Trail of about half a mile to the viewpoint only. The Riverside Walk is a little longer. Car parking and toilets are available.

From Rogie Falls it is approximately 22 miles and 35 minutes driving time to get back to Inverness.

ORKNEY MAINLAND (SIDE TRIP)

We had decided to incorporate a trip over to mainland Orkney into our North Coast 500 itinerary. It's easy to do, and a relatively short crossing from either Gills Bay (with Pentland Ferries) or Scrabster (with Northlink Ferries).

If you take a trip out to any of the islands, please do allow some contingency for any potential weather-related disruptions or cancellations. On the day we were due to return all three of Pentland's sailings were cancelled due to adverse weather. As Northlink use a different route, we managed to get on to their afternoon sailing instead, but even that was under review for a time.

It is worth recommending that should you travel on Northlink Ferries, it is worth considering paying the extra (currently £7.50 per person) to use the Magnus Lounge. For this, you get free drinks (soft, alcoholic and teas & coffees) and a range of snacks such as fruit, crisps, Orkney fudge, biscuits, scones, pastries etc. It is also located at the centre of the ship, where there is less motion. We were surprised to find only about 4 other people using the lounge!

When you arrive in Orkney, try to visit the tourist office when you arrive and pick up their extremely useful maps of the West and East mainland. These maps are really helpful and show where all the tourist attractions are, with a short description of each.

In Kirkwall, there is plenty of accommodation. If you are looking for a campsite or somewhere cheap to stay, then we would recommend the Orkney Caravan Park at the Pickaquoy Centre: http://orkneycaravanpark.co.uk/ They take tents, caravans and motorhomes and also have camping pods available for a good price. We stayed in one of the pods for our first night. Thereafter we stayed near Birsay in the north of the mainland (the amazing lodge we stayed at is recommended at the end of this guide).

Orkney is known for having some of the best-preserved prehistoric sites in Europe, so if that is of interest to you, you will have plenty of them to visit! There are also many walks, which can often be a little scary as they pass beside sheer cliffs. Finally, we also enjoyed some canoeing in our inflatable double canoe that we had brought with us.

We have split this section of the guide book into the following categories:-

ARCHAEOLOGICAL AND HISTORIC
WALKS
WILDLIFE
CANOEING
TOURS AND TASTINGS

ARCHAEOLOGICAL AND HISTORIC

ST MAGNUS' CATHEDRAL, KIRKWALL

The main historic landmark in Kirkwall, the cathedral was founded in 1137 by the Viking, Earl Rognvald and is dedicated to the Earl of Orkney, Magnus Erlendsson. It took about 300 years to finish building the cathedral.

BISHOP'S AND EARL'S PALACES, KIRKWALL

Found next to St Magnus' Cathedral, the Bishop's Palace was built about the same time as the Cathedral, with The Earl's Palace being added much later, around the early 17th century.

THE ORKNEY MUSEUM, KIRKWALL

Admission to the museum is free. Among other things, it houses many artefacts from the island's prehistoric and medieval past. The museum is housed in Tankerness House, an A-listed building, on Broad Street close to St Magnus Cathedral.

ITALIAN CHAPEL, LAMB HOLM

This Roman Catholic chapel sits on the island of Lamb

Holm, which is connected to mainland Orkney by one of the Churchill Barriers. It was constructed by Italian POWs during the Second World War. It was built from two Nissen huts joined together. There is a small admission fee.

EARL'S PALACE AND ST MAGNUS' CHURCH, BIRSAY

The Earl's Palace is reckoned to have been built around 1574 by Earl Robert Stewart. Only the ruins remain.

The nearby St Magnus' Church stands on the site of a much older church, which was in existence long before St Magnus' Cathedral in Kirkwall. The church has been rebuilt and restored several times.

BROUGH OF BIRSAY, BIRSAY

A small island accessible on foot by a tidal causeway. You can explore the Pictish, Norse and Medieval remains and take a walk to the lighthouse looking out to the Atlantic ocean. Admission fee to the archaeological site applies.

SKARA BRAE & SKAILL HOUSE, SANDWICK

Both included on the one admission ticket, Skara Brae is one of the main archaeological attractions on Orkney, a Neolithic settlement around 5,000 years old. The remains were unearthed after a storm back in 1850. It lies on the grounds of Skaill House, a historic mansion house built in the 1620s.

While you are there, you may want to allow yourself some extra time to enjoy a walk along the sandy beach at the Bay of Skaill, right next to Skara Brae. Look out for the Hole O'Row, a sea cave worn through the headland.

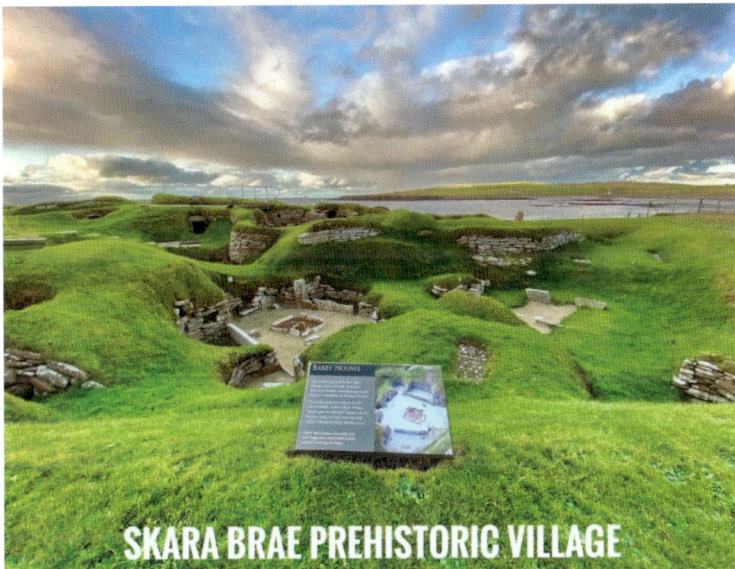

SKARA BRAE PREHISTORIC VILLAGE

MAESHOWE, STENNESS

A chambered tomb built around 5,000 years ago. The entrance passage is aligned with the setting of the midwinter sun so that it shines down the passage to illuminate the tomb's interior.

Please note that visits are by guided tours only, departing from the Maeshowe Visitor Centre at Stenness. Phone 01856 851266 or Email customer@hes.scot or visit the website for details and booking - https://www.historicenvironment.scot/visit-a-place/places/maeshowe-chambered-cairn/

BROCH OF GURNESS, AIKERNESS, EVIE

The iron-age broch village here is considered the best-preserved of all broch villages. The actual broch (a large stone tower) stood at the centre of the village and probably housed the head family of the community. An entrance fee applies.

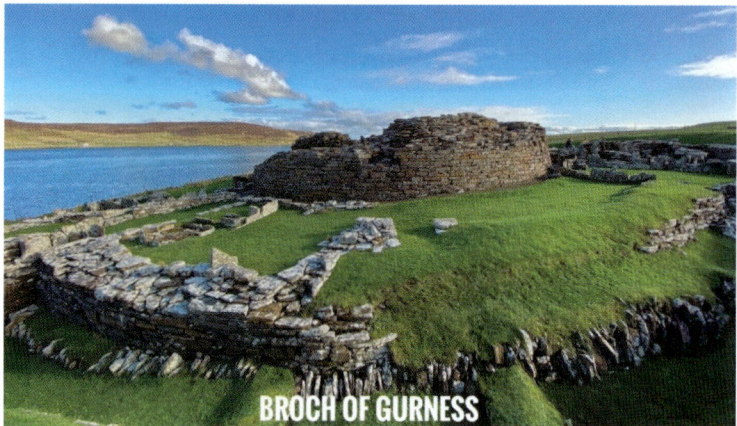

BROCH OF GURNESS

CHURCHILL BARRIERS

These causeways help to make up mainland Orkney by

linking the north mainland with Burray, South Ronaldsay, Lamb Holm and Glimps Holm. They were built during the second world war to protect the anchorage at Scapa Flow, after an attack by a German submarine. Most of the work was done by the Italian POWs who were held in the camp at Lamb Holm.

RING OF BRODGAR STONE CIRCLE AND HENGE, STENNESS

A Neolithic ceremonial site consisting of a large stone circle and prehistoric burial mounds. The stones are surrounded by a large circular ditch.

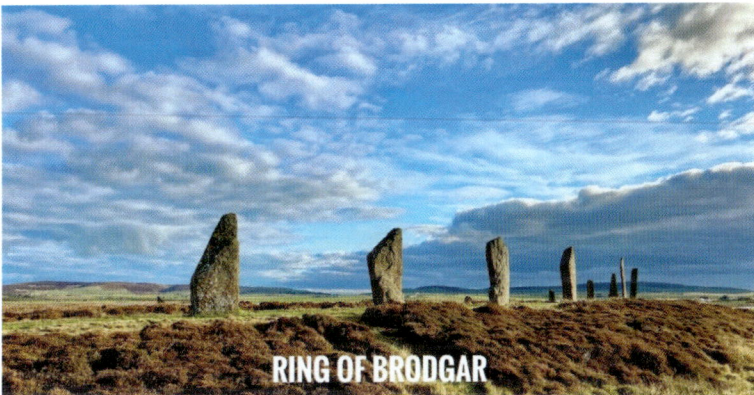

RING OF BRODGAR

STANDING STONES OF STENNESS

Around a mile from the Ring of Brodgar, you will come across the Neolithic Stones of Stenness. Only 4 of the original 12 stones remain, the highest being around 6 metres tall. Over 5,000 years old, this is believed to be one of the earliest stone circles in Britain.

WALKS

YESNABY COASTAL WALK AND SEA STACK

Part of a longer walk from Stromness to Birsay, most people park in the small car park at Yesnaby and head south to do a return walk out to the Yesnaby sea stack (commonly called Yesnaby Castle), a sea stack with a natural arch at its base.

In autumn we found this walk very muddy and were glad of our welly boots! Needless to say, be careful when walking near the cliffs. The return walk was perhaps two miles.

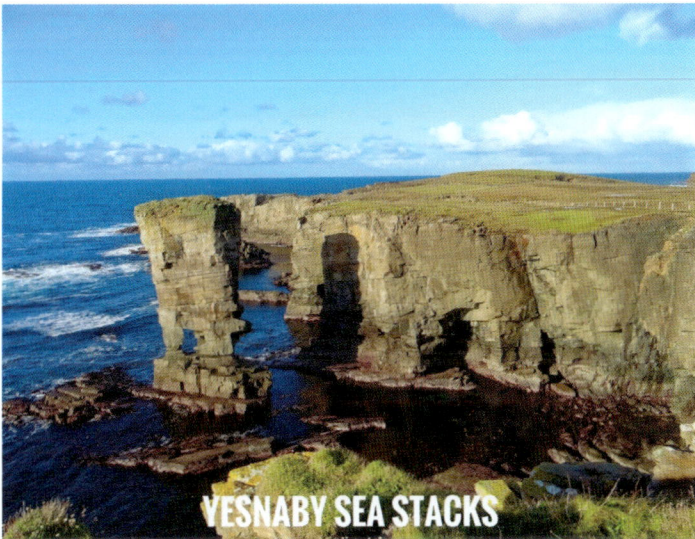

YESNABY SEA STACKS

THE GLOUP AND MULL HEAD RESERVE, DEERNESS (EAST MAINLAND)

The Gloup is a spectacular collapsed sea cave. It is about 80 feet deep and is separated from the sea by a land bridge. To get to the Gloup it is a very short walk from the car park.

Mull Head Nature Reserve has circular walks of up to around 4 miles; please take great care when walking near the cliffs. You can walk onto the Brough of Deerness, though great care is needed on the narrow exposed path. We chose not to do this part of the walk as it looked too scary!

If you do make it to the Brough, there are some remains of an old Viking settlement at the top.

WILDLIFE

WINDWICK BAY, SOUTH RONALDSAY (EAST MAINLAND)

If you are visiting Orkney between October and December, head out here to view the seal pups. It is probably the best place on the island to see them.
There is a small parking bay overlooking the beach. Bring some binoculars for a better view.

The scenery is also great, with cliffs and sea stacks. There is a path that goes along the top of the sea cliffs, just a little uphill from the car park, but care is needed.

MARWICK HEAD RSPB RESERVE

A must-do for birdwatchers, the car park at Marwick Head is about 11 miles north of Stromness. The best time to view the sea birds on the cliffs is between April and July and in summer you may be lucky enough to see a puffin.

CANOEING

CHURCHILL BARRIERS SHIPWRECK

An excellent place to canoe and likely to be reasonably calm in good weather. You can paddle around the shipwreck at Churchill Barrier 3 for a closer look. Easy access from the sandy beach.

CHURCHILL BARRIERS

AIKERNESS BEACH (NEAR BROCH OF GURNESS)

A lovely bay near the Broch of Gurness, with beach access. Unfortunately on the day that we planned to canoe here, the weather had turned and a storm was heading in, so we went to the Highland Park Distillery instead!

A couple of days before that it looked very calm, but it's always best to check with the locals and be aware of the tides to be safe.

LOCH STENNESS AND LOCH HARRAY (WEST MAINLAND)

Both of these lochs have access from the road. Loch Harray can be beautiful at sunset.

TOURS AND TASTINGS

ORKNEY BREWERY

Just a mile from Skara Brae, the Orkney Brewery is housed in a former Victorian schoolhouse. Their beers are popular and certain ones sell in the big supermarkets. Tours are available, which include 3 samples in the Tasting Room afterwards. The Tasting Hall and Cafe are in what was formerly a classroom. Meals and snacks are available.

Normally closed for the winter, so check first if travelling in the off-season.
Phone 01856 841 777.

HIGHLAND PARK DISTILLERY, KIRKWALL

The Highland Park Distillery was founded over 200 years ago and has been legally distilling whisky for almost 200 years. They make exceptionally popular single malts.

A variety of tours and tastings are available, the basic tour currently costs £15 per person. When we took the tour it included two tastings and you got to keep your glass as a souvenir.

Tours are available all year round.

ORKNEY WINE COMPANY, LAMB HOLM

Producing vegan-friendly, sulphur-free fruit wines and liqueurs. Their shop and tasting room is next to the Italian Chapel.

We were offered a tasting of a variety of their wines, liqueurs and rum and ended up buying their 2014 "Black Portent". The tastings were free and there was no hard sell afterwards.

DEERNESS DISTILLERY, NEWHALL, DEERNESS (EAST MAINLAND)

Producing award-winning vodka and gin, this distillery has a shop and offers tours and tastings. The shop and tasting room are open from April to September. Tours are available by appointment; phone 01856 741264 to arrange.

POPULAR CAMPSITES

Bearing in mind that things do change, at present unless indicated, some of these campsites are closed during the off-season. Check the websites for accurate opening and closing times, but as a rough guide generally, they tend to be open from around March/April – September/October. This list is not exhaustive, but we have included many of the more popular overnight stops.

DORNOCH (NEAR DUNROBIN CASTLE):

Dornoch Caravan and Camping Park -
http://dornochcaravans.co.uk/
Phone: 01862 810423
Email: info@dornochcaravans.co.uk

BRORA:

Brora Caravan Club Site -
https://www.caravanclub.co.uk/club-
sites/scotland/highlands/brora-caravan-club-site/
Phone: 01408 621479
Email: UKSitesBookingService@camc.com

JOHN O' GROATS / GILLS BAY:

John O' Groats Caravan and Camping Site -
https://www.johnogroatscampsite.co.uk/

Phone: 01955 611329 or 01955 611744
Email: info@johnogroatscampsite.co.uk

Stroma View Caravan and Camping Site (open all year) -
http://stromaview.co.uk/
Phone: 01955 611313
Email: john@stromaview.co.uk

Ferry View Night Stop (open all year) -
https://www.ferryview.scot/
Phone: 07799 147 146 or 07717 497 396
Email: info@ferryview.scot

DUNNET HEAD / DUNNET BAY:

Dunnet Bay Caravan Club Site -
https://www.caravanclub.co.uk/club-
sites/scotland/highlands/dunnet-bay-caravan-club-site/
Phone: 01847 821319
Email: UKSitesBookingService@camc.com

Morven View Caravan Site (open all year) -
http://www.morvenview.com/
Phone: 01955 66 1222
Email: info@morvenview.com

DURNESS:

Sango Sands Oasis Campsite (open all year, however, in
the off-season, the only facilities are water fill-up and

electric hook-up. Note the toilets and showers are closed in the off-season and you need to use the public toilets beside the shop nearby) - https://sangosands.com/
Phone: 07838 381065 (use the online form or email to book)
Email: stay@sangosands.com

SCOURIE:

Scourie Caravan and Camping - https://www.scouriecampsitesutherland.com/
Phone: 01971 502060
Email: info@scouriecampsitesutherland.com

LOCHINVER AREA:

Shore Caravan Site, Achmelvich - http://shorecaravansite.yolasite.com/
Phone: 01571 844393
Email: sazmacleod@hotmail.com

Clachtoll Beach Campsite - https://www.clachtollbeachcampsite.com/
Phone: 01571 855377
Email: warden@clachtollbeachcampsite.com

ULLAPOOL:

Ardmair Point Touring Caravan and Camping Park - http://www.ardmair.com/caravan.html

Phone: 01854 612054 or 07814 260514
Email: sales@ardmair.com

Broomfield Holiday Park - http://www.broomfieldhp.com/
Phone: 01854 61 2020
Email: sross@broomfieldhp.com

GRUINARD BAY:

Gruinard Bay Caravan Park (they also have tent pitches) -
http://www.gruinardbay.co.uk/
Phone: 01445 731556 / 07972 614532
Email: stay@gruinardbay.co.uk

POOLEWE:

Inverewe Gardens Poolewe Camping and Caravan Club Site
-
https://www.campingandcaravanningclub.co.uk/campsite
s/uk/highlands/achnasheen/inverewe-gardens-poolewe-
camping-and-caravanning-club-site/
Phone: 01445 781249
Email:
membershipservices@campingandcaravanningclub.co.uk

GAIRLOCH:

Sands Caravan and Camping Park -
https://www.sandscaravanandcamping.co.uk/
Phone: 01445 712 152

Email: info@sandscaravanandcamping.co.uk

SHEILDAIG:

Sheildaig Camping and Cabins -
https://www.shieldaigcampingandcabins.co.uk/
Phone: 01520 755224
Email: shieldaigcamping@gmail.com

APPLECROSS:

Visit Applecross Campsite (also takes motorhomes and
caravans)-
https://visitapplecross.com/accommodation/camping/
Phone: 01520 744268
Email: enquiries@visitapplecross.com

RECOMMENDED ACCOMMODATION

Although we haven't included any accommodation listings in this guide, below are some of the places we stayed that we feel were particularly outstanding and/or good value and therefore worth a mention.

It is also worth mentioning that in Lochinver if you fancy a bit of pampering, there are several places with hot tubs, though some have a minimum stay policy. The one we stayed in was nice, but many of the others also looked great. Most are on Booking.com, so the best idea is to search for your dates and see what is available.

DUNNET BAY – DUNNET BAY ESCAPES: We loved the beautiful spacious garden suite, superb breakfast and use of a hot tub (which due to our unfortunate late arrival we didn't use).

Tip: Also check their prices on Booking.com, as we got a really good offer there when we booked.
Website: dunnetbayescapes.com

DURNESS – AIDEN HOUSE SHEPHERD'S HUTS: Beautifully decorated with everything you need including a kitchen, spacious en-suite, dining area and decking outside.
Website: https://www.aidenhouse.co.uk/shepherd-huts-durness-nc500/

APPLECROSS – HARTFIELD HOUSE: A good budget option, this hostel has private rooms (not en-suite) as well as dormitories, a nice lounge and a big kitchen/dining room.

Tip: Again, it is worth comparing the price of this hostel on Booking.com. We got a slightly cheaper price there but had to pre-pay.
Website: https://www.hartfieldhouse.org.uk/

ORKNEY MAINLAND – GRUKALTY SELF-CATERING:
Stunning and very comfortable lodge with 2 double bedrooms, a large lounge/kitchen/dining room and a hot tub with a view!
Website: https://www.grukaltyorkneyselfcatering.co.uk/

We hope this short guide has been useful in helping you to plan your North Coast 500 trip and that you have a fantastic time.

On occasion, we have mentioned checking out the Walk Highlands website for more detailed information on walks which we have recommended. Their website address is https://www.walkhighlands.co.uk/ and we find them to be one of the best walking route websites we have come across.

If you enjoyed this guide, please feel free to follow us on Facebook – our page is called Exploreourworld.

Several of our photos are available to purchase as canvas or prints on the following websites:
http://photo4me.com/profile/ycarroll
https://tinyurl.com/YCarroll

We also have a website Exploreourworld.home.blog which you may enjoy browsing and a YouTube channel ExploreOURWorld.

Printed in Great Britain
by Amazon